To my husband Jaekeun Cho who,
along with his family, taught me Korean culture.
—Tina Cho

To my parents Bilquis and Ashraf,
thank you for showing me the world.
— Farida Zaman

Korean Celebrations

Festivals, Holidays and Traditions

text by **Tina Cho**

illustrated by **Farida Zaman**

TUTTLE Publishing

Tokyo | Rutland, Vermont | Singapore

Welcome to Korea!
Hwan-young-ham-ni-da 환영합니다

Holidays and festivals are a great way to experience Korean culture—and they're fun! Ancient traditions are very important to the huge number of people who live on this small peninsula in Asia. Colorful clothing and tasty foods rich with meaning are found in major celebrations. In this book you can see how important days are celebrated in Korea, make some Korean food, play a traditional game or two, and learn some Korean language. Are you ready? *Gap-shi-da!* Let's go!

What Do We Celebrate?

Korean celebrations are based on religion, superstition, seasons and a hard-won freedom. Some traditional celebrations date back to the time before the Three Kingdoms period (57 BCE—668 CE) but only a handful of these are still celebrated today. Seasonal festivals are important to this farming country, and some of the best-loved festivals celebrate the coming of the next new season. Beliefs also influence holidays and festivals here. Both the birth of the Buddha and the birth of Jesus have a place in Korean holidays. Because of a history filled with Japanese rule, and other conflicts in the last century, some of the holidays we celebrate today are about our joy and pride in Korea's freedom as an independent country.

Korea uses two calendars—the **solar calendar** like countries in the Western Hemisphere and the **lunar calendar**. The lunar calendar is used for traditional holidays, birthdays, and deaths. It is based on the eight phases of the moon. The new moon is the first day of the lunar month. China also uses the lunar calendar.

What Do We Wear?

Koreans wear *hanboks* during weddings and major traditional holidays such as the New Year and Thanksgiving. Hanboks are a loose-fitting, flowing outfit that date back to the Three Kingdoms period. In those days, common people wore white hanboks while the people in the upper classes wore colorful ones. Women embroidered on them to show their love for their family members. There are different styles of hanboks to suit the age of the wearer and the event that's being celebrated.

Koreans wear hanboks 한복...

short jacket
jeogori 저고리

overcoat
po 포

skirt
chima 치마

pants
baji 바지

socks
beoseon 버선

New Year's Day Sinjeong 신정

January 1st

Ring in the New Year in Seoul, South Korea's capital! People gather in Jongno, a historic street in Seoul, at the Boshingak Belfry. The city puts on a ceremony along with the traditional ringing of this massive bell. City officials, along with some selected citizens, get the honor of ringing it. The bell is rung thirty-three times. Long ago during the Joseon Dynasty, the bell was rung thirty-three times at 4 a.m. and twenty-eight times at 10 p.m. The bell signaled the opening and closing of the four main gates to the city. Fireworks light the sky as Koreans celebrate the New Year.

The Lunar New Year Seollal 설날

1st Day of the 1st Lunar Month

Sae-hae-boke-mahni-paduh-sayo or Happy New Year! This is one of Korea's biggest traditional holidays. In fact, it's a three-day holiday! The Lunar New Year is the first day of the first lunar month. Women prepare food and *hanboks*, for this special day. You must look your best, especially by wearing new clothes. Roads are busy as people travel to their hometowns to be with parents and other family members. Ancestral rites, bowing for blessings, eating, and playing games are some of the many activities of this traditional holiday.

Ancestral Rites Charye 차례

The morning begins with families honoring their ancestors. They bow and offer special prepared foods on a low table to the spirits of their ancestors. Some believe that the ancestors return to enjoy the food and bless the coming year.

Bowing for Blessings Saebae 세배

Children and even their parents pay respect to their elders. They kneel and bow on the floor. Family members say special wishes to each other. Children receive money from their grandparents, parents, aunts, and uncles.

Holiday Foods! Mandu and Dduk Guk 만두 떡국

Seollal is a time to enjoy lots of special foods. Dumplings called *mandu* are a traditional favorite that you will see at many special holidays. Usually the whole family helps make the dumplings. *Mandu* can be boiled, fried, or made into a soup. *Dduk Guk*, which is rice cake soup, is another New Year favorite. The thin cakes are shaped like coins, so it's thought that eating this soup will bring prosperity in the new year. According to the Korean aging system, once you have eaten your *Dduk Guk*, you have turned a year older.

Gifts Seonmul 선물

Family members give practical gifts to each other. Stores sell gift sets of shampoo, soap, fruit and more. These gifts are wrapped in silky cloths to be carried to the relative's home. For example, you could receive a big box of twenty Asian pears. A sweet, healthy, and expensive gift! Children often have beautiful silk bags to hold the money given to them by elders.

Games Go-stop 고스톱

Go-stop is a card game that uses flower cards from Japan. The goal of the game is to match four cards of the same months with a small amount of points.

Seesaw Neolttwigi 널뛰기

Seesaw or *Neolttwigi* is a traditional women's game. A board is laid across a straw bag, and the women stand up on each end. One woman jumps on the board while the other one sails up high. The woman who loses her balance first loses the game.

Kites Yeon 연

Flying kites and kite fighting are popular with children during Seollal. Korean kites are rectangular, made from traditional paper and bamboo sticks. Long ago kites were used by the military for giving secret instructions to the soldiers. Today children like to fly kites in parks by the rivers.

7

A Favorite New Year Game Yut-nori 윷놀이

Yut-nori, a popular traditional game, is played with four carved sticks and a game board. Players toss the sticks and earn points depending on how the sticks land. Here's how you can make and play you own *Yut-nori* game.

WHAT YOU NEED
black marker
4 popsicle sticks
I sheet of white paper
I penny
I dime

1. Using the marker, draw 3 X's on the front of the sticks. Draw a "B" on the back of only I stick.

2. Game board: Draw a large circle on the paper. Divide the circle into quarters. Draw 4 smiley faces where the lines connect, plus I smiley face in the middle.

3. Between each section of the smiley faces, draw 4 dots along the circle. In the middle, draw 2 dots between each smiley along the lines.

4. Write "START" at the bottom smiley face.

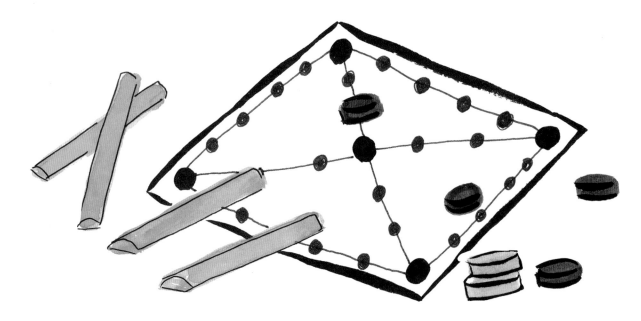

This is what a traditional board looks like.

How to play: This game is usually played by two teams.

Goal: To move your marker all the way around the circle. Points are earned by how the sticks fall. If the X's are showing, the stick is face up. If the X's are not showing, then the stick is face down.

1. The first person throws the sticks in the air. They move their marker (penny or dime) according to the following point system:

    1 stick face down = move 1 space, called a pig or *doh*

    2 sticks face down = move 2 spaces, called a dog or *gae*

    3 sticks face down = move 3 spaces, called a sheep or *geol*

    4 sticks face down = move 4 spaces, called a cow or *yut* + go again

    4 sticks face up = move 5 spaces, called a horse or *mo* + go again

    If the stick with the "B" is showing, that person moves their marker 1 space backwards on the board.

    If the person's marker lands on an opponent's marker, they move their opponent back to start and go again.

2. The first person on the opposite team throws the sticks and moves their marker.

3. Plays continue around the board. If a person lands on a smiley face, they have the option of a shortcut back to START by using the steps in the middle.

4. The first team with their marker back to START wins the game!

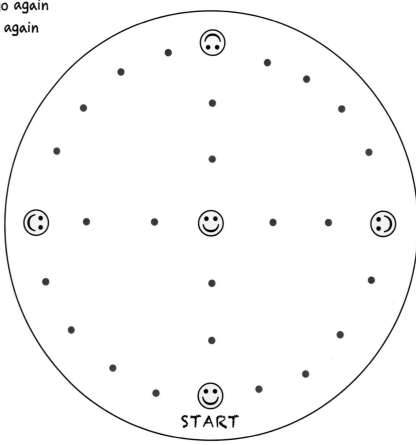

First Full Moon Daeboreum 대보름

The 15ᵗʰ day of the 1ˢᵗ Lunar month

Long ago farming was the main job in Korea, and so the people prayed to the moon for abundant harvests at the beginning of the New Year. The moon represented the goddess of earth. A great harvest meant a good life that year. Celebrate the first full moon with traditions that wish happiness and health for all.

Eating Nuts Bureom 부럼

The morning begins by cracking nutshells such as walnuts, chestnuts, and pine nuts with their teeth. The amount of nuts eaten is according to one's age, and they try to crack the nut on the first try for good luck. Wishes are shouted for peace and health. Some believe this strengthens their teeth and prevents skin allergies for the coming year.

Buy My Heat Deowipalgi 더위팔기

As a practical joke, Koreans like to sell their upcoming summer heat to their neighbor. They go to a friend's house early in the morning and call out the friend's name. If the friend replies, "Yes"or "Hello," the first person says, "Buy my heat!" Then it's believed that your neighbor accumulates all your heat for the summer plus his own. But if you call out your friend's name, and your friend catches you first by replying, "Buy my heat," then you accumulate your friend's heat plus your own. Nowadays instead of walking to the friend's house, people text it on their cell phones!

Rice with Veggies Okokban 오곡반

On this day Koreans eat *Okokban*, or five-grain rice and seasoned vegetables. They often share it with other families to bring good luck and the nutrients make the summer heat easier to take.

Twirling Fire Jwibullori 쥐불놀이

A fun nighttime activity is *jwibullori*. While the banks of dried rice paddies and fields from the fall season are burned to get rid of insects and mice, people twirl cans with lit kindling inside them. The cans are full of holes, so the spinning cans make a miniature light show.

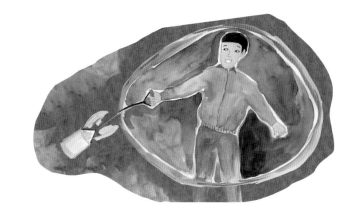

Bridge Walking Daribapgi 다리밟기

Daribalgi is when Koreans walk back and forth on a bridge under the full moon to bring good health to their legs. The number of bridge crossing equals one's age. If you're nine, you'd cross the bridge nine times. Another interpretation is that twelve crossings will bring twelve months of good health.

Circle Dance Ganggangsullae 강강술래

Women's circle dance or *Ganggangsullae* is performed by many women holding hands in a big circle under the moon. One woman starts the song and the others join in and sing "Ganggangsullae" at the end of each verse. The dance starts slowly and then gets faster and faster as the women lift up their voices to the moon and express their emotions of sorrow and regret. This is a time for women to forget their troubles and have fun in a cooperative beautiful way.

Independence Day Samiljeol 삼일절

March 1st

On this day Koreans celebrate independence from Japan. In 1910, Japan forced Korea to live under its rule. The Korean people were only allowed to speak Japanese. They were given Japanese names, and all Korean culture and traditions became illegal. Secretly, Koreans preserved their culture, and on March 1, 1919, thirty-three nationalists met in Tapgol Park in Seoul. They read a declaration of independence from Japan. Their efforts did bring about some changes in the way Japan controlled Korea, but Japan continued to rule Korea until 1945.

Now this day is an official holiday. Flags are flown, and a bell ceremony is held in Seoul at the Boshingak Belfry. The same bell that rings in the new year is rung thirty-three times to remember the thirty-three nationalists.

Korean National Anthem: Aegukga 애국가

Aegukga means the song of love for the country. These are the words in English.

Until the East Sea's waves are dry, and Mt. Baektusan worn away,
God watch o'er our land forever! Our Korea manse!

CHORUS
1. Rose of Sharon, thousand miles of range and river land!
Guarded by her people, ever may Korea stand!

2. Like that Mt. Namsan armored pine, standing on duty still,
wind or frost, unchanging ever, be our resolute will.

3. In autumn's, arching evening sky, crystal, and cloudless blue,
Be the radiant moon our spirit, steadfast, single, and true.

4. With such a will, and such a spirit, loyalty, heart and hand,
Let us love, come grief, come gladness, this, our beloved land!

Days of Love

Valentine's Day 고스톱

February 14ᵗʰ

Women give chocolates or other gifts to men.
Some make their own chocolates using candy molds.

White Day 화이트데이

March 14ᵗʰ

Men give women candy, usually not chocolate.
This day originates from Japan where a candy
company started Marshmallow Day in 1978,
producing marshmallows for gifts of love.

Black Day 블랙데이

April 14ᵗʰ

Young singles eat black-bean noodles (*jajang*) 자장
together to show they are mourning for love.

Buddha's Birthday Seokga Tansinil 석가탄신일

April 8th Lunar Calendar

This is a national holiday to celebrate the founder of one of Korea's main religions. Colorful lanterns are strung across streets close to temples for many weeks. The lanterns symbolize wisdom, bringing light to the world. A Lotus Lantern Festival is held in which brightly lit lanterns are paraded down the street.

Children's Day Orini-nal 어린이날

May 5th

Imagine a holiday just for children! Korean kids get to stay home from school and celebrate with their parents and grandparents at parks, museums, and zoos. Some receive gifts and go on special outings. The idea for Children's Day originated from Bang Jeong-hwan, a children's writer. On May 1, 1923, she wrote a letter to adults about speaking softly and with respect to children because they are the future of the nation. She said that children who grow up without respect will disrespect others. During the Japanese rule of Korea, the elders were depressed about the future of Korea. They were hopeful that their children would have a better life. In 1946, the date of Children's Day change from May 1st to May 5th. One banner in a parade read, "Children are the nation's flowers." Vendors fill the street with balloons, candy, popcorn, and even small pets, all for the purpose of praising and encouraging children.

15

Parent's Day Ubbai-nal 어버이 날

May 8th

In Korea, moms and dads are celebrated on the same day. Thank your parents for all they've done for you on Parent's Day! Red carnations are given to parents along with money or gifts carrying a wish for good health, such as a massage or spa treatments. Many families take their parents out to dinner. Why not surprise your parents with a carnation made by you?

Folding a Paper Carnation Jongi-chubgi 종이 접기

WHAT YOU NEED

3 × 3 inch (8 × 8 cm) piece of red or pink origami paper
3 × 3 inch (8 × 8 cm) piece of green origami paper
Scissors

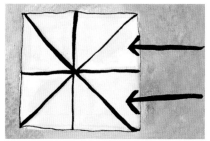

3. Open it and bring the other pair of opposite corners together to form another triangle. Your paper should have these criss-crossed lines.

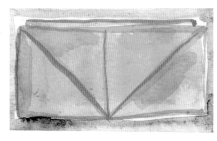

I. FOR THE FLOWER, fold the paper in half to make a rectangle. Open it and fold it the other way to make another rectangle.

4. Look at the two diagonal lines on the right side. We're going to push the middle part in and bring those two diagonal lines together.

2. Open it and bring opposite corners together to form a triangle.

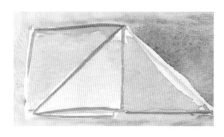

5. Now do the same thing to the other side. Push the middle part in and bring the two diagonal lines together.

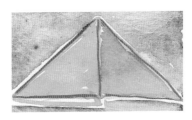

6. You'll end up with a double-layer triangle like this.

7. Now turn it so the point is toward you. Then cut a scalloped line at the top.

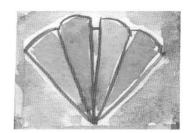

8. Now bring the left corner of the top petal and fold it to the middle line.

9. Then do it to the other side. Now your carnation is finished.

10. FOR THE LEAVES, do the same steps using the green paper but don't cut a scalloped line. It will look like this:

11. Now take the left top corner that you brought over, and fold it down to make a leaf.

12. Then do the same with the right one.

13. Now flip the paper over, and you'll see a triangle. Take the left side and fold it to the middle line.

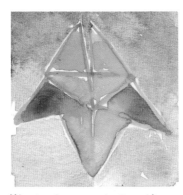

14. And repeat for the right side.

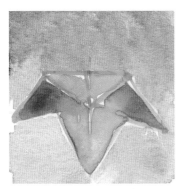

15. Turn the paper back to the front.

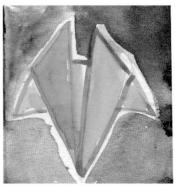

16. Fold those top triangles behind the leaves so they don't show.

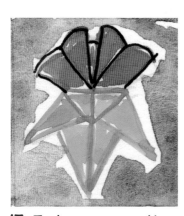

17. Tuck your carnation into the middle of the leaf stem. You're finished!

The warm weather brings three patriotic holidays to Korea.

Memorial Day Hyeongchun-il 현충일

June 6th

This is a lot like Memorial Day in many parts of the world. Flags are flown at half-staff on this national holiday, and silent prayers are said at 10 a.m. for the soldiers who died in all of Korea's wars. A large ceremony is held in the National Cemetery in Seoul.

Constitution Day Jeheonjeol 제헌절

July 17th

On July 17, 1948, the first constitution of the Republic of Korea was established. The constitution has been changed nine times.

Liberation Day Gwangbokjeol 광복절

August 15th

South Koreans celebrate the official end of Japanese colonization by flying the Korean flag.

Japan surrendered to the United States marking the end of World War II on August 15, 1945. However, the northern and southern halves of Korea were divided. The Soviet Union set up a communist government in the north, and the United States military supported the south. On August 15, 1948 the Republic of Korea (South Korea) was established. September 9, 1948 the People's Republic of Korea (North Korea) was announced. The communist north built up its army and invaded South Korea on June 25, 1950. A three-year war was fought along the 38th north latitude. A ceasefire was signed on July 27, 1953.

Korea's flag is full of meaning. The white background represents purity and peace. The red half of the circle represents positive forces, while the blue half represents negative forces. Together, they represent balance and energy. The sets of lines at the four corners are called *trigrams*. Each represents a natural element, a season of the year, a virtue and other things as well. Together, the four trigrams suggest balance and completeness.

Korea's national flower is the *mugunghwa* 무궁화 (hibiscus syriacus). In English it's called the Rose of Sharon. One reason for the choice is that it is a flower that can withstand a great deal, and survive even when it has been harmed, just as the Korean people have done throughout centuries of struggle.

A Celebration of Summer Dano 단오
5th day of the 5th Lunar month

With the heat of summer comes another celebration—Dano! Farmers finished with spring planting could now relax and watch their crops grow. The summer rainy season spread disease and sicknesses, and so the people practiced superstitions which they believed would bring good health. They thought a date in which the month and day had the same number, such as May 5th or June 6th were especially lucky days. The Dano festival is held for a whole month!

Swinging Geunettagi 그네타기

How high can you swing? A woman or girl stands on a wooden swing and sometimes rings a bell that is hung from the top. The highest swinger wins.

Hair Washing Danojang 다노장

With this superstition, women shampooed their hair with the juice of iris leaves and even drank it to ease headaches—and also to have softer hair.

Wrestling Ssireum 씨름

In this game, one person tries to throw the other to the ground by grabbing his waist and thigh.

Fans Buchae 부채

Long ago the royal court made fans for the king, and the king distributed them to the people for the coming summer. Folded fans beautifully decorated are still popular. Here's how to make one of your own.

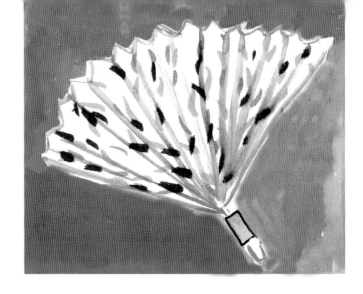

1. Lay the two sheets of paper next to each other lengthwise like a long hot dog.

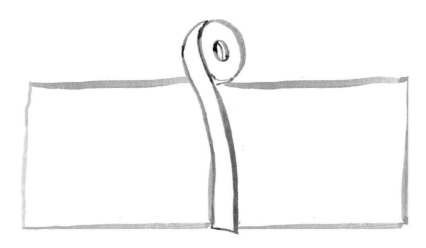

2. Tape them together along the "seam."

YOU WILL NEED

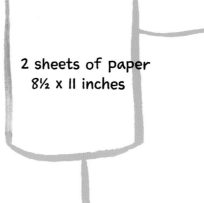

2 sheets of paper
8½ x 11 inches

Marker Pens

Tape

1 strip of colored paper
1 x 3 inches

22

3. Many fans bought in today's Korea markets have beautiful or fun patterns on them. Use your markers to a pattern on your fan.

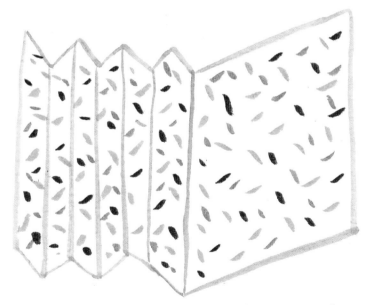

4. Turn your long paper so that the short end is next to you. Start folding the paper—fold up about an inch, then flip the paper to the back and fold up. Continue this pattern until you're at the end.

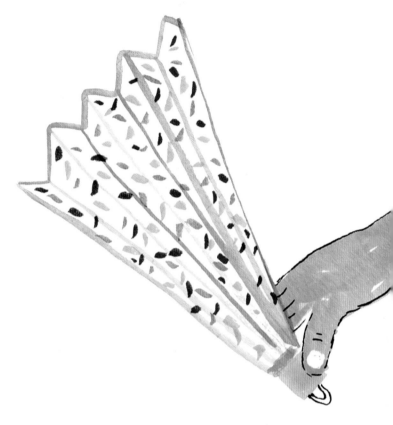

5. Wrap your strip of colored paper around the bottom of your fan. This is where you'll hold the fan. Tape the strip on. Now your fan is ready to keep you cool!

A Festival of Love Chilseok 칠석

7th Day of the 7th Lunar Month

An ancient legend says that long ago there were two lovers in heaven. Jiknyeo, a weaver maid and daughter of the Lord of Heaven, fell in love with Gyeonu, the son of a farmer who lived east of the Milky Way. Jiknyeo stopped weaving hemp cloth, and Gyeonu stopped farming so that they could spend time together. Because of this the crops in heaven were neglected. The Lord became angry and ordered Jiknyeo and Gyeonu to live at opposite ends of the heavens. They could meet one night each year, on Chilseok. Crows and magpies built a bridge for them by leaning together. The rain that falls on Chilseok is said to be the happy tears of the two lovers, and the continued rain is their tears of sorrow after being separated for another twelve months.

Stitching and Weaving Cheon-eul jjada 천을 짜다

Girls stitch and weave hemp cloth on Chilseok to remember Jiknyeo.

Wheat Pancakes Miljeonbyeong 밀전병

Eating wheat pancakes is popular on Chilseok because the monsoon rains would ruin the stored wheat as the weather also became chilly.

Thanksgiving Day Chuseok 추석
15th Day of the 8th Lunar Month

The Thanksgiving harvest takes place under a full moon and begins the night before with the making of *songpyeon* or half-moon shaped rice cakes, seasoned with pine needles. On the morning of Chuseok, some families clear weeds from the graves of ancestors. And similar to the Lunar New Year, they offer food and bow to their ancestors' spirits. Families share a meal together including the freshly, harvested rice. Games are played outside such as tug of war, *ssireum* wrestling, and *Ganggangsullae*, the circle moon dance by women.

Half-moon Rice Cake Songpyeon 송편

Everyone in Korea looks forward to eating *songpyeon* on Chuseok. This is an easy recipe. It has a couple of unusual ingredients, like pine needles and frozen rice flour, but the yummy results are worth the extra effort of gathering the ingredients together and kneading the dough.

YOU WILL NEED
Long pine needles washed and dried,
   Chestnuts (optional)

NOTE: Before you start, be sure to ask your parents for their permission and supervision!

I bag of frozen rice flour from
   an Asian Grocery store

Salt

Brown sugar

I cup of boiling
water

ALSO HAVE READY
a couple of cooking pots
I steamer
I nut/seed grinder
I tea towel
I piece of cheesecloth big
   enough to line your steamer
an assortment of bowls
I plate or cookie pan for the
   last step
I small basting brush
   (optional)
I plate for serving your
   songpyeon

Sesame seeds

Sesame oil

Honey

28

How to Make Them

1. Pour 1 cup (160g) of rice flour in a bowl and mix with 3 tablespoons of boiling water.

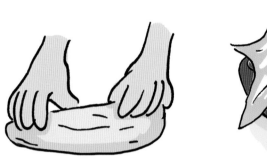

2. Mix and knead the dough until it no longer sticks to your hands. Keep the dough covered and slightly moist.

3. Time to make the fillings. **For a sweet sesame filling:** Grind ¼ cup (37.5g) of sesame seeds.

4. Add 1 tablespoon (12.5g) of brown sugar and 1 tablespoon (about 21 grams) of honey.

5. For the chestnut filling: Boil 10 chestnuts.

6. Peel the skins. Cut the nuts into small pieces. Mix with a little salt and sugar.

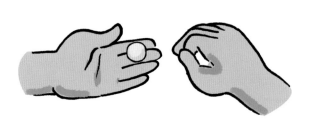

7. Make 1 inch balls from the dough.

Looks like this!

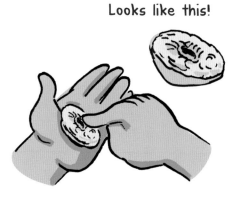

8. Use your finger to make a bowl.

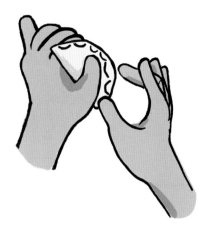

9. Add one of the fillings into the bowl. Pinch the two sides of the dough together. Press to make a half-moon shape. Lay it on a plate.

10. STEAM THE SONGPYEON:
Boil water in a steamer.

11. Add cheesecloth or a wet towel in the steamer. Lay pine needles on the bottom and then a layer of songpyeon with another layer of pine needles on top.

12. Boil for 20-30 minutes. Drain and rinse with cold water.

13. Use your hands or a pastry brush and apply a small coating of sesame oil to each songpyeon.

14. Lay them on a bed of pine needles and enjoy. This is a basic recipe, and the cakes will be a soft white in color, but in Korea it's common to make dough in different colors, using natural ingredients to tint the different batches (for example, a little blueberry juice to make light purple dough, or raspberry juice to make pink dough).

National Foundation Day Gaecheonjeol 개천절

October 3rd

The founding of Korea is based on a unique myth dating back to 2333 BCE.

The Lord of the Heavens had a son who was displeased about how the people on earth were living. He asked his father if he could go down and rule over them. His request was granted. The son, named Hwanung, was given three thousand servants along with three lords. He landed in modern day North Korea on Mt. Taebak and set up a kingdom. One day a bear and a tiger approached him.

"Could you please make us human?" they asked.

"Here are twenty garlic cloves and a handful of the mugwort herb. Eat only this for one hundred days, pray to the gods, and your wish will be granted."

The tiger and bear went inside a cave, prayed, and ate bits of the food. But the days were long, and the tiger grew hungry and impatient. So he left. The bear stayed, and on the tweny-first day, it turned into a beautiful woman. Hwanung married her, and they had a son named Dangun.

In 2333 BCE, Dangun established a new kingdom which he named Asadal, which was later changed to Choseon also called Gochoseon. The legend says he ruled for fifteen hundred years.

So the Korean people celebrate the founding which might have occurred over forty-three hundred years ago.

Hangeul Day Hangeul-nal 한글날

October 9th

Can you write in Korean? This alphabet was created by King Sejong the Great. Before the 1400s, Koreans used Chinese characters, but this writing was difficult for people to learn. King Sejong and his scholars invented an easier alphabet based on sounds. Each of the twenty-four letters stands for one sound. The new language, Hangeul, has ten vowels and fourteen consonants. Because it's an easy writing system, almost all Koreans can read and write! On Hangeul Day, writing-related events are held along with tributes to King Sejong.

세종 대왕

You can try reading Korean, too.

Consonants	ㄱ	ㄴ	ㄷ	ㄹ	ㅁ	ㅂ	ㅅ	ㅇ	ㅈ	ㅊ	ㅋ	ㅌ	ㅍ	ㅎ
	g	n	d	l, r	m	b, p	s	ng	j	ch	k	t	p	h

Vowels	ㅏ	ㅑ	ㅓ	ㅕ	ㅗ	ㅛ	ㅜ	ㅠ	ㅡ	ㅣ
	ah	yah	uh	yuh	oh	yo	oo	yoo	eu	ee

The letters read from left to right just like English; however, they also go top to bottom to form syllables.
For example, if we spelled "cat" the Korean way, it would be ca
t.

Can you figure out this word? 곰 It's pronounced "gome," which means "bear."
And one more... 친구? This is pronounced "cheen-goo," which means "friend." See how there are two syllables?
One more thing, sometimes consonants are doubled for a greater emphasis on the sound, like this word: 토끼
This says "toe-ggee," meaning "rabbit."
Great! Now you're ready for some more words!

Hello, how are you?	An-nyung-ha-say-o?	안녕하세요
good-bye	An-nyung-hee-ga-say-o	안녕히가세요
yes	Nae	네
no	Ah-nee-yo	아니요
mom	Uhm-ma	엄마
dad	Ahp-pa	아빠
thank you	Kam-sa-hahm-nee-da	감사합니다
please	Jae-bal	제발

35

A Sweet Celebration Pepero Day

November 11th

If you're in Korea on November 11th, you'll notice students handing out boxes of the famous Pepero chocolate stick cookies to their friends. This isn't really a holiday, just a popular celebration for young people that spread in 1994 when some girls in a southern city of Korea gave boxes of Pepero cookies to friends. Pepero Day is held on November 11th since the date is made of four straight lines, just like the cookies. You can give homemade Pepero treats to your friends, too, by using this simple recipe.

YOU WILL NEED
Big pretzel sticks
Bag of chocolate chips
Jimmies or other colorful
  sprinkles

YOU WILL ALSO NEED
Double boiler or a
  microwave and a deep
  microwave-safe bowl
Plate
Waxed paper

NOTE: Before you start, be sure to ask your parents for their permission and supervision!

HOW TO MAKE THEM
1. Lay a sheet of wax paper out on your plate
2. Melt the chocolate according to the package directions in the microwave or a double boiler.
3. Dip each pretzel about ⅔ to ¾ of the way into the bowl and lay on the waxed paper.
4. Scatter some sprinkles over your homemade Pepero.

You can do this with any baking chips from the baking section of your store, including white chocolate chips, butterscotch chips, caramel chips, and more. (You can melt a little food coloring into white chocolate chips to add color to your dip.) The combination of sweet and salty tastes great!

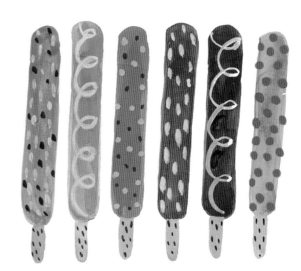

Winter Solstice Dongji 동지

December 21st or 22nd

On this longest night of the year, Koreans eat *patjuk*, a red-bean porridge which some believe drives away evil. This day was also called "little new year's day," since the days that follow it become gradually longer, bringing a new year, and a new spring.

Christmas Seogntanjeol 성탄절

December 25th

Christians celebrate the birth of Jesus on December 25th, just like other countries in the world. Some families put up a tree, and some businesses decorate with lights. Christmas in Korea is considered a romantic as well as a family holiday, so going out on Christmas is a popular activity. Being together is important for families too, and of course, family members and couples enjoy giving gifts to one another.

Birthdays Saeng-il 생일

In Korea, certain birthdays are especially important, remembering a time when life expectancy was short. People live long, healthy lives now, but birthdays that mark important milestones are still loved and celebrated.

100 Days Baek-il 백일

When a baby is one hundred days old, a small feast is held. Long ago before modern medicine, many babies didn't live past 100 days. To celebrate this happy day, special rice cakes are eaten that symbolize a long, healthy life, a good mind, and pure spirit. The family also gives away 100 rice cakes to family and friends which is believed to bring long life to the baby.

1ˢᵗ Birthday Dol 돌

Happy Birthday, Baby! A huge banquet is given with many guests. The child wears a special *hanbok* and hat. A table is prepared with special foods of fruit, rice cakes, fish, and other dishes. Family and friends give money or gold rings to the child. The most exciting part is when the child selects an item to foretell his or her future. A tray of items is put in front of the child such as string to represent long life, a pencil to represent a life as a scholar, and money to represent a life of wealth. The child is encouraged to grab something from the tray so the parents can see what the future holds. Will the child be intelligent? Wealthy? Live a long life?

60ᵗʰ Birthday Hwan-gap 환갑

Living to be sixty was rare long ago, so sixty was once considered to be a very old age. Today, life expectancy is longer, and sixty isn't old at all, but this birthday is still a special one, and people still enjoy the Hwan-gap of family and friends. The children of the parent bow in order of age. Sometimes poems and songs are shared. Another reason sixty is such an important number is that it's also the number of years in the lunar calendar cycle

Weddings Gyeolhon 결혼

Western Style Weddings

Before the wedding, the bride and groom will meet their new families, and the families will meet each other. Gifts are exchanged between the bride and groom and between the families. The bride and groom usually get married in a wedding hall or church just like a Western-style wedding. The groom walks down the aisle first. The bride walks down with her father. Everyone claps. After the ceremony the families may have a small private ceremony before enjoying a huge banquet with all their guests. Guests give money to the couple.

Traditional Weddings

Some couples choose a traditional Korean-style wedding. In this type of wedding, the bride and groom wear special hanboks and headpieces. They perform many deep bows to each other and their parents to show respect. The groom gives the bride's family a pair of wooden geese. This means he will be loyal to his wife. A ceremony of drinking from two halves of a gourd symbolizes the belief that, together, they are one. After the wedding, there's a little parade in which the bride rides in a *gama*, a chair carried on poles, while the rest of the wedding party walks. In the olden days, the wedding took place at the bride's home, and the groom rode his horse or walked there. After three days at her family's house, the groom would walk, and the bride rode to the groom's family's house.

Local Festivals

Just like in most other parts of the world, different regions and cities in Korea have their own local celebrations. Here are just some of the many festivals all around Korea.

Ice Festival Hwacheon Sancheoneo 화천 산천어

What do you do with too much snow and ice?
You can attend winter festivals! People ice fish,
play ice soccer, view snow sculptures, and sled.
When the Hwacheoncheon Stream in Gangwon-do
freezes in the winter, everyone comes out to carve
holes in the ice and fish for the breed of salmon
called *sancheoneo*.

Andong Mask Festival

You can learn Korean culture by watching traditional mask dances, pantomime, and marionettes in the Andong region during this ten-day festival in September and October. These dances portray folk stories. Artists from other countries also participate.

Mask Dance Andong 안동

Mask dances are a cherished tradition in many parts of Korea. The masks followed specific designs, and were traditionally made of wood, papier mache or gourds. At one time, it was a custom in most regions to burn the masks after the performance and make new ones for the next.

Green Tea Festival Boseong 보성

Have you ever had green tea? This festival is held in one of the largest tea plantations in Korea. You can tour the tea fields, pick tea leaves, make tea, and enjoy many other activities.

Ginseng Festival Geumsan Insam 금산 인삼

Each October, farmers in Geumsan are thankful for the ginseng harvest and celebrate with a festival. People can learn about the health effects of ginseng, take a ginseng footbath, and watch traditional performances.

Rice Festival Icheon 이천

One of the best places to buy rice is from Icheon. The rice of Icheon has been served to Korea's kings and is still prized. At this festival you can learn how to thresh rice, watch a rice parade, and taste freshly cooked rice from a huge iron cauldron.

Mud Festival Boryeong 보령

Do you like to play in mud? If so, this festival is for you! The mud at Daecheon Beach is rich in minerals and healthy for your skin. At this festival, there are plenty of mud activities that are fun ways to give yourself a mud bath, like mud skiing, mud slides, mud painting and more!

Cherry Blossom Festival Jinhae Gunhangje 진해 군항제

This is South Korea's most popular place to admire cherry blossoms, but blossom-viewing is enjoyed in other Korean towns and cities as well. Walk down a street or over a bridge surrounded by pink and white cherry trees!

Horizon Festival Gimje 김제

This late September through early October festival celebrates Korea's farming culture. It takes place near the Byeokgolje Reservoir, in Gimje, an area known for its rice crop. Twin dragons lead the evening's torchlight parade, and the festival is full of cooking, music and friendly tug-of-war and other competitions.

Firefly Festival Muju 무주

To see the magic and beauty of fireflies, you must travel to the city of Muju, where the air is clean and conditions are perfect for these insects to live. Lots of cultural activities will keep you busy and light is celebrated in many ways as light-filled lanterns and balloons light up the sky.

Published by Tuttle Publishing, an imprint of
Periplus Editions (HK) Ltd.

www.tuttlepublishing.com

Text © 2019 Tina Cho
Illustrations © 2019 Farida Zaman

Isbn: 978-0-8048-4694-3

Library of Congress Control Number: 2019935467

DISTRIBUTED BY

North America, Latin America & Europe
Tuttle Publishing
364 Innovation Drive
North Clarendon VT 05759-9436 U.S.A.
Tel: 1 (802) 773-8930
Fax: 1 (802) 773-6993
info@tuttlepublishing.com
www.tuttlepublishing.com

Asia Pacific
Berkeley Books Pte. Ltd.
3 Kallang Sector #04-01
Singapore 349278
Tel: (65) 6741 2178
Fax: (65) 6741 2179
inquiries@periplus.com.sg
www.tuttlepublishing.com

First Edition
23 22 21 20 19
10 9 8 7 6 5 4 3 2 1

Printed in China
1904RR

ABOUT TUTTLE:
"Books to Span the East and West"

Our core mission at Tuttle Publishing is to create
books which bring people together one page at
a time. Tuttle was founded in 1832 in the small
New England town of Rutland, Vermont (USA).
Our fundamental values remain as strong today
as they were then—to publish best-in-class
books informing the English-speaking world
about the countries and peoples of Asia. The
world has become a smaller place today and
Asia's economic, cultural and political influence
has expanded, yet the need for meaningful
dialogue and information about this diverse
region has never been greater. Since 1948, Tuttle
has been a leader in publishing books on the
cultures, arts, cuisines, languages and literatures
of Asia. Our authors and photographers have
won numerous awards and Tuttle has published
thousands of books on subjects ranging from
martial arts to paper crafts. We welcome you to
explore the wealth of information available on
Asia at **www.tuttlepublishing.com**.